BRITAIN IN OLD PH

C000000674

AROUND SEDGLEY

TREVOR GENGE

ALAN SUTTON PUBLISHING LIMITED

Alan Sutton Publishing Limited
Phoenix Mill · Far Thrupp · Stroud
Gloucestershire · GL5 2BU

First published 1995

Copyright © Trevor Genge, 1995

Cover photographs: *(front) staff of the sub-post office, High Street, Sedgley, early this century; (back) a class party at Lanesfield Board school, 1953.*

British Library Cataloguing in Publication Data.
A catalogue record for this book is available from
the British Library.

ISBN 0-7509-0844-0

Typeset in 9/10 Sabon.
Typesetting and origination by
Alan Sutton Publishing Limited.
Printed in Great Britain by
Hartnolls, Bodmin, Cornwall.

The parish church of All Saints, Sedgley, is on an ancient foundation. A church has stood on this site since Norman times, at least, and names of clergy are known from 1184. As late as 1829 it was the parish church and the only church for the whole manor of nine villages, except for a chapel of ease at Lower Gornal, built in 1817. The church was rebuilt in 1829 and its present tower contains within it an earlier tower.

Contents

Introduction

The name Sedgley is Saxon in origin and means the clearing made by Secga in the large midland forest and heath. Yet it was the Norman and medieval barons that shaped the manor and established the territorial boundaries that were to survive into the late nineteenth century.

Nine distinct villages made up the manor and they were all served by the one parish church of All Saints in Sedgley village. At least two, Sedgley and Ettingshall, are named in William the Conqueror's Domesday Book of 1086; a third name, Catspelle, may refer to Cotwall End. The nine of the final union were Sedgley, Woodsetton, Nether or Lower Gornal, Ouvre or Upper Gornal, Cotwall End, Gospel End, Ettingshall, Brierley and Coseley. Modern Ettingshall has now moved northwards, with the building of Ettingshall New Village, in the nineteenth century, outside the old manor boundary. Upper Ettingshall is the southern end of the land area that was the original village. Its old northern boundary was at the road now designated the A4039. Brierley occupied part of the area now known as Bradley: the latter too is mentioned by name in the Domesday Book.

At the tithe survey of 1844 the nine villages were still effectively units, though with many smaller hamlets springing up between them. All were overseen by the Local Boards operating under the auspices of the parish. These were the forerunners of the Urban District Councils which resulted from the Local Government reforms of the late nineteenth century.

Interestingly the castle, now named Dudley, falls within the lands of the village of Woodsetton and might, more accurately, be described as Sedgley castle after the ancient manor. In the past the castle was always listed as a Staffordshire castle, while Dudley was an island of land belonging to Worcestershire.

The limestone ridge that runs from the castle northwards through Wrens Nest, Mons Hill, Hurst Hill and the Beacon has always provided a spine to the manor. To the east the land was very much influenced by the industrial revolution and falls within the Black Country, while to the west a large proportion of the area remained as farm land until the middle of this century. Mutual interests kept the two halves together. The cottage industries springing from the Black Country iron works spread across the ridge to the west; the farmers helped supply the needs of the rapidly growing industrial population to the east; and the limestone ridge enjoyed the double purpose of providing lime for the fields and flux for the furnaces.

It was the mineral wealth that was to determine the area's future. The famed 'Ten Yard' coal seam often had ironstone lying in an adjacent layer. Both could often be taken from the same working and so near to the surface was this layer that the operation could take place in daylight. One of the sites where this occurred was the enormous opencast mine at Parkfield, now the site of the GKN laboratories on the A4123. Fireclay abounded for furnace linings and the limestone provided the final ingredient: the flux which assisted the smelting process by separating the impurities from the iron.

Iron working came to the area early: Sedgley nails were used by Archbishop Cranmer in the building of Hampton Court. Transport was difficult and those nails travelled by pack horse to Bewdley, were transported down the River Severn and then transferred to ships that sailed around the south coast and up the Thames to Hampton Court.

Field enclosure also arrived early in Sedgley. A great land survey of 1614 gives field names that were still appearing on the 1844 tithe schedule. Some are still identifiable today. The shape of the boundary hedges of some of the surviving fields also reveals that they were taken from original woodland and not merely enclosures of existing land.

In common with much of the Black Country, many small farms or smallholdings continued to exist amongst the pits and ironworks of the area. They made patches of green amongst the engulfing grey-blue banks of colliery spoil and the heaped ash of the furnaces. The ruthless extraction of coal resulted in much subsidence to houses and other buildings and, in some cases, temporary realignment of roads was not unknown in order to be able to extract the precious commodity. Although all in one parish, the individuality of the villages seems to have survived until the late 1950s, when extensive new house building began to join the villages and hamlets into one. The most drastic change was seen when the farms and fields on the western slopes of the Beacon were lost.

Early road communication within the area was poor and, to begin with, Sedgley's industrial goods were satisfactorily transported by canal. Designed by James Brindley, this first had a winding course from Wolverhampton, through Brierley and on towards Wednesbury before returning to the manor near Bloomfield. Later Thomas Telford designed the improvements, part of which was a tunnel under Coseley, opened in 1837, drastically reducing the length of Brindley's canal.

By this time, however, turnpike roads had appeared in the manor: in 1842 twelve toll houses served these roads. The Red Lion, in the Bull Ring, was the coaching inn with provision for the changing of horses. Railways too were on the horizon.

This still left many smaller hamlets linked by only the roughest of tracks. Many of the ancient field paths, or bier ways, are still discernible leading to the parish church.

During the 1880s and 1890s steam trams (a tramcar drawn by a separate steam locomotive) were in use but were not popular. Electric trams arrived in 1901, the same year that they were introduced by London United Tramways in the Hammersmith and Shepherd's Bush area of London. The trams passed from Bilston, along the manor boundary, to the Fighting Cocks inn. There they turned for Sedgley and onwards to Dudley.

From feudal times the area would have been governed from the manor court, first at the castle, and later from the Lord's courthouse in the village of Sedgley. This became the Court House Inn where the manor court met until 1925, though from a much earlier date refreshments had been obtainable!

The boom years of the Industrial Revolution saw a considerable increase in the population. In 1801 the Sedgley area had a recorded population of 9,874: by 1851 it was 29,447. Incomers arrived from surrounding counties to feed the demands of the growing labour-intensive industries.

Census returns show the different villages to have been quite self-sufficient, having their own local shoemakers, soap boilers, candle makers, etc. The Gornals also had a wider part to play in the local economy as the source of the much-used commodities of Cheshire salt and local sand.

Although only one is clearly identified there were several bull rings in the area. Coseley had its own as did Lower Gornal. In time the cruel sports of bull baiting and dog fighting gave way to more humane pastimes. Pride was still taken in dogs and their breeding, however, and is still evident today.

Musicianship seems to have become a source of village pride and also, no doubt, the source of rivalry between local bands. Home brewing was another popular occupation and left the area with an abundance of public houses well into this century.

Churches and chapels spread, to meet the needs of growing local populations, from the late seventeenth century, but particularly throughout the whole of the nineteenth century. Some of these religious bodies opened schools before the 1870 Education Act and, afterwards, the Board schools were also placed strategically throughout the area. Both types of schools continued for many years.

Some indication of the difficulty of managing such a large and growing area can be seen first in the administration of the land east of the Beacon separately as Lower Sedgley (later to become Coseley UDC). With local government reform at the end of the nineteenth century and the introduction of urban district councils to replace the old Boards this area was renamed after one of its own villages, Coseley.

As well as changes to the village administration came the development of the larger factory units of this century and the reduction in the cottage industries of the past, although some persisted until quite recently. The opening of the Birmingham New Road in 1927 (A4123), by the Prince of Wales, made a further divisive impact upon the area, also leading to much ribbon development along its length. Finally, the absorbing of the old Sedgley lands into the two Metropolitan boroughs of Wolverhampton and Dudley would have seemed the death knell to all the former allegiances. Yet village loyalties are still discernible as are the old village and hamlet centres.

Change has not always been rapid and the work of the early photographers allows us to recreate a picture well beyond the immediate past. It is difficult to name our first local photographer, but evidence points strongly to Egginton the Chemist as one early recorder of Sedgley village events with the new medium. It is also fortunate that John Price, printers of Bilston, considered parts of the area beautiful enough, or curious enough, to warrant a postcard series.

The local archive collections of both Dudley and Wolverhampton Boroughs and the Black Country Society, together with the Sedgley Local History Society and Museum, have all contributed valuable pictures or information. What has also been discovered is the array of material still resting in private hands and now in evidence here.

Section One

AROUND THE
BULL RING

Sedgley Drug Stores.

The Bull Ring, 1930s. The name Bull Ring refers to the cruel sport of bull baiting which would have been staged here. It probably continued here for hundreds of years until the middle of the nineteenth century. The heart of the manor naturally formed close to the ancient church. Close by were the village green, the main well, and the stocks which reputedly stood in a position now occupied by the shops to the right in the above scene. At that time J.T. Egginton's premises occupied only the tall building in the centre (see page 9), while next door but one is A. Sproson Vinrace's grocery store. Sandwiched between is a little shop that was created from a former house. It is often recalled as a greengrocers but obviously sold tobacco products as well. The little low wall seen up Dudley Street was the village pinfold or pound. This was not the only site in the manor where dogs were set on tethered bulls for sport. There were at least two other bull rings, one at Lower Gornal and the other at Coseley.

Egginton's ambitions were finally realised when the whole block became something of a small multiple store, including café. The modern ground-floor frontage, completed in about 1960, was the final addition. The whole site was cleared shortly after this photograph of 1971.

This delightful seventeenth-century stone dwelling at the corner of Dean Street (well below road level) was also partly incorporated into Egginton's and not only housed the dispensary, but also a branch of Repairwell cleaners. Photographed in 1968, it stood round the corner to the right of the buildings shown above.

The Bull Ring under snow, looking north, 1890s. This shows Hilton's house, facing the road, and, on the far left, the workshop and entrance to the yard of the building firm Hilton & Caswell. Behind it, in the distance, is the inappropriately named Manor House, which it never was. On the right, the one building standing at this time, is an old farmhouse, now the site of the Penny Farthing Arcade.

The Georgian façade of the Court House Inn conceals a more ancient stone building which was, in reality, the manorial court house. Its use would have begun when the feudal practice of holding court at the castle ceased. Although it became an inn during the nineteenth century, if not earlier, it was obviously dual purpose, for the last court case was heard there as late as 1925.

This unusual view has been taken from an upper floor window of Egginton's, early this century. It is one of the indications that Egginton took a practical interest in photography. It shows the only early nineteenth-century buildings remaining in today's Bull Ring. The lady in full skirt heads for Zebulon Butler's Fancy Repository. The tradesmen's carts are in the Red Lion yard.

Zebulon Butler's Fancy Repository, c. 1900. See previous picture: the Red Lion is revealed, as is also the High Street. The shop to the right is Roden's. Bread and cakes were sold, and bread was delivered in a large, wheeled basket cart, which was pushed around the village.

A Wednesday afternoon at the turn of the century. Sheep and cows are being driven through the Bull Ring from Wolverhampton market.

The Red Lion, late 1960s. This was Sedgley's coaching inn. Coaches paused here en route from Wolverhampton to Dudley and the south. Another route went through Himley to Worcester. This photograph shows that the front door had been moved off centre, where it would have been in 1750. It has since been moved again, this time to the left.

FARMS & FARMING

Haystack close to the centre of Sedgley. Gate Street

lies behind. The young lady on the ladder is a

member of the Fellows family who farmed there.

Haymaking group, 1900. A typically rural scene in Dukes Meadow, off Ettymore Road, Sedgley. Even so, at this time, many cottage industries must have been close at hand. Many of the great farmhouses of the manor survived into the twentieth century, by which time some were over four hundred years old. Although on the western side of Sedgley Beacon agricultural lands predominated, it was quite common to find a small farmhouse, with its fields, existing amongst the pits and forges to the east. The eastern slopes of the beacon itself were extensively farmed from Ettingshall Park, and the land was ploughed almost to the top of the ridge. Evidence of the medieval ridge and furrow ploughing system can still be found within the fields of Gospel End and Cotwall End.

Sedgley Hall. Repairs to a gable in 1951 (below) revealed that a much earlier timbered construction had been hidden by a nineteenth-century modernisation. Reference to the house was made in a land survey of 1614, at which time it was the seat of the Jevon family. It was the home of Stephen Wilkes in 1924 (see page 31). The Hall was demolished in 1966 to make way for a modern housing estate of that name, although the site still remains undeveloped land to this day.

Cotwall End House, Catholic Lane (formerly Downing's Lane). The Downings, who gave their name to the lane, lived at the bottom of it in this house. Its demolition in 1961 was a tragic loss, as the beautiful gable reveals. Fortunately after its demolition the lands were retained and are now open to the public as the Cotwall End nature reserve.

In fields behind Cotwall End House was the Whit Well, photographed in the 1970s. In recent times it was still possible to see cows gathered at this ancient and valuable Sedgley spring.

One of two stone barns that served Cotwall End House. The use of Gornal stone was extensive throughout the manor, not only for houses and farm buildings, but also field walls. Before 1850 both Sedgley and Ruiton would have been built almost completely of stone. The evidence of this is now fast disappearing, although the Gornal stone field walls persist in places both inside and beyond the manor.

Ruiton farm, Upper Gornal, 1963. Though of more modest proportions than Cotwall End House, this has its own charms. Mainly an early stone building it had later additions including the Victorian porch with its cast iron window frame.

Ruiton Windmill, 1950s. Also of local stone, though of a later date than the farm, it had a predecessor memorialised in a local inn sign as The Old Mill. The new mill, shown here with the last remnants of its sails, is now shorn to a stump, but happily is preserved as a centre for scouting activities. From the west it remains a landmark on the horizon.

Conqueror's Farm, Lower Gornal, *c*. 1910. Great pride of place is shown by this family, probably the Caswells, who pose outside. Even the horses are brought into the picture, together with farmhands. The Caswells had many interests in Sedgley, including a smaller farm in Catholic Lane. The photograph shows that the building was strengthened against subsidence by tie bars and corner plates. The farm was demolished in 1962.

Abbey Farm, Abbey Street, Lower Gornal, 1970. It owed that name to the fact that the income from some, or all, of its lands was once dedicated to one of the local Midland abbeys. In 1842 it was the home of a local doctor, Dr Hicken.

High Arcal Farm, Woodsetton, 1953. A stone-built seventeenth-century farmhouse with a porch, it is reminiscent of the Yorkshire Dales. The farm served the Parliamentary forces during the siege of Dudley Castle. It was known at an early date as Flaxhall's tenement.

Robert's Green Farmhouse, Lower Gornal, 1963. It was on the corner of Robert Street and Jews Lane.

Red Lane Farm, Gospel End, 1975. This tiny farmhouse is near the junction of Red Lane with Gospel End Road. Replaced by a modern bungalow to its west, it survived into the late 1970s; in its final years it was a store for baled straw (see page 58).

$\int$EDGLEY $\int$ARVEST-$\int$OME $\int$ESTIVAL, 1873.

ORDER OF PROCEEDINGS FOR THE DAY.

1.0 p.m.   The Farmers and Labourers will assemble in the Infant School Room, Sedgley, and walk in Procession to the Church, where DIVINE SERVICE will be held, and a Short Sermon will be preached by the Vicar: After Service, the Procession will re-form and March through the Village, headed by MESSRS. PARKES' DRUM AND FIFE BAND, kindly lent for the occasion, to Turls' Hill; where, at

2.0 p.m.   DINNER will be provided in a Tent.

3.30 to 6 p.m.   GAMES and ATHLETIC SPORTS.

5.0 p.m.   TEA for Women.

6.0 p.m.   Bread and Cheese and Beer will be given to the Men, at the Tent.

6.30 p.m.   Fireworks, &c.

There will be an EVENING SERVICE in the Church, for all who like thus to conclude the day, at 8 p.m.

ORDER OF ATHLETIC SPORTS.

N.B.—None but Farm Labourers having tickets for the dinner, will be allowed to compete; they must give their names before starting, to MR. W. HUGHES, the Secretary

No one will be allowed to take more than two prizes.

1. Flat Race, 100 yards.
2. Hurdle Race, 6 flights, 80 yards.
3. Long Jump.
4. Racing in Sacks.
5. Flat Race, 200 yards.
6. Hopping Race, 50 yards.
7. Climbing a Greased Pole.
8. Flat Race, ¼ mile.
9. Wheelbarrow Race, blindfold.
10. High Jump.
11. Throwing the Hammer.
12. Second Sack Race.

13. Consolation Stakes, for those who have not won any Prize, 150 yards Flat Race.

A Prize of 2s.6d. will be given to Winner in any of the above Competitions, except the ¼ mile race which will be 5s., and climbing the greased pole, on which will be placed a Leg of Mutton.

N.B.—Visitors will be admitted to the grounds at 3.30 p.m. to witness the Sports, &c., on payment of 3d. each.

HINDE, STEAM PRINTER, DUDLEY STREET, WOLVERHAMPTON.

A harvest festival handbill reveals much of the form of celebration in Sedgley in 1873. The original possessor of the handbill has ticked off the sporting events he wished to enter!

THE INDUSTRIAL
PAST

Miners at Baggeridge.

Lime burning, Round Hill Quarry, Sedgley Beacon, early this century. The Beacon monument can be seen on the horizon. The quarry was mentioned in Dr Robert Plots *The Natural History of the County of Stafford* (1686). Dr Plot was the first keeper of the Ashmolean Museum, from 1683 to 1690, and was Historiographer Royal in 1688. Lime was used as an iron-smelting flux, but also in building and in farming. Hilton & Caswell builders owned this limeworks (their yard was in the Bull Ring). Industry thrived in an area so rich in mineral resources.

A disused lime kiln, Wrens Nest, Woodsetton, 1970.

Sandstone crushing, Ruiton, Upper Gornal, 1930s. Mr Charles Harper is seen behind the horse, which turns the grinding wheel, while his niece Matilda Harper pushes the wheelbarrow. Sand was used for house flooring and for cleaning table tops.

The Round House, Ruiton, 1960s. Sand crushing, seen taking place in the open air above, could also be undertaken in shelter in the Round House or sand mill. The practice had ceased long before this photograph was taken.

Open cast mine, Coseley, *c.* 1890. The presence of the famous Ten Yard coal seam, so close to the surface, was not just a vital raw material for the Sedgley area but for the whole Black Country. Here the great seam is laid bare in the open cast mine near to St Chad's. Coseley windmill can be seen to the right of the church.

An engraving from a late nineteenth-century book, *Earth's Riches*, by E.W. Payne. He describes the great Parkfield Colliery in Ettingshall as having coal and ironstone lying together in bands, and all worked 'in the light of day'. This is now the site of the GKN Laboratories on the Birmingham New Road.

Old gin pit, Claycroft, West Coseley. A geological survey of 1926 speaks of a seam of coal 39 ft 5 in thick here.

ETHERIDGE & SON,

57, Hurst Hill, nr. Bilston.

COAL, COKE and LIME MERCHANTS.
Wholesale and Retail.

Dealers in all kinds of

CANNOCK CHASE COALS, Etc.

SPECIAL PRICES for TRUCKS or BOAT LOADS SENT TO ANY STATION or WHARF.

Coal Wharf and Lime Works: DEEPFIELDS.

BEST HOUSE COALS A SPECIALITY.

Etheridge & Son of Hurst Hill advertise their wares, 1911. Coal merchants were numerous, supplying the domestic market.

They even had their own personal railway trucks. As they had a wharf at Deepfields, Coseley, they used Deepfields railway station on the LNWR line. At that time the station was situated at the end of Havacre Lane.

The Baggeridge 'Sinkers', *c.* 1902. In 1895 Herbert W. Hughes, mining engineer to the Earl of Dudley, predicted that coal could be found on the western side of Sedgley Beacon. It took a deep mine to reach it, but in 1902 the famous 30 ft seam, the 'thick' coal, was located at Baggeridge, Gospel End.

Miners working in the thick coal seam at Baggeridge.

A pit pony draws tubs in Baggeridge pit.

Stephen Wilkes' warehouse, Brick Street. Wilkes was one of the successful Sedgley nail factors. He was also a Congregationalist and used the building as an evening school for young men from 1837. His stone-built warehouse, erected in about 1830, is now used by Cottage Blinds; it also houses Sedgley's own local museum.

TRADE S.W.   MARKS.

STEPHEN WILKES,

SEDGLEY, NEAR DUDLEY,

MANUFACTURER OF THE

BEST BEST S.W. HORSE NAILS,

Best Best Brazil Mule Shoe Nails,

AND ALL KINDS OF

WROUGHT NAILS,

SPIKES, RIVETS, TACKS,

GALVANIZED NAILS, CHAINS, STAPLES, &c., &c.

A typical Wilkes advertisement, showing the trade marks. It is taken from a trade directory of 1874.

B. & W. Waterhouse's screw factory and manager's house stood on the corner of Hollywell Street and Hurst Hill (previously Can Lane, Ettingshall). Hurst Hill sub-post office operated from the little cottage on the left of the frontage and was still in use when this photograph was taken in 1970. The post office counter has now been transferred across the road to modern shops.

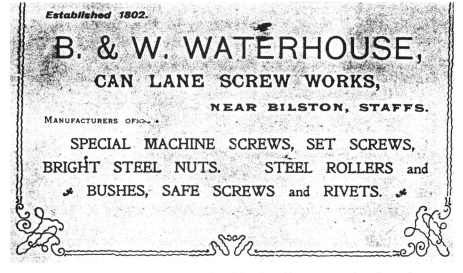

Established 1802.

B. & W. WATERHOUSE,

CAN LANE SCREW WORKS,

NEAR BILSTON, STAFFS.

MANUFACTURERS OF

SPECIAL MACHINE SCREWS, SET SCREWS, BRIGHT STEEL NUTS. STEEL ROLLERS and BUSHES, SAFE SCREWS and RIVETS.

A Waterhouse advertisement showing the old style address. It is taken from the Hurst Hill Methodist Chapel bazaar programme of 1911.

A stone-built nailshop in Wakelam's Fold, Lower Gornal.

A row of nailshops, Brick Street, Sedgley, 1960s. They were situated opposite the Wilkes warehouse (see page 31). One of them had become a little cobbler's. They were demolished shortly after this photograph was taken; the site is now a car park.

Domestic nailshop, just off the Bull Ring, Sedgley, 1971. It was originally stone built, but has been much repaired.

A collection of nail makers' tools and various nails, discovered in Lower Gornal in the 1960s. The worn hammer shaft says much about the grinding hardship of local industry and local thrift!

James Marsh (1825–1922) was the last nailer in Lower Gornal. Here Mr Marsh holds a length of iron in his hand. After heating the end in the hearth (constructed from local stone fragments), he would have moved to his anvil to make the nail. Many nailers had a mechanical hammer called an 'Oliver', which was operated by foot pedal. Others worked only by hand. The gleam at the top right of the picture is from his bottle of cold tea. The photograph must have been taken at his nailshop in Hopyard Lane, towards the end of his working life.

Parkfield Ironworks. The front furnace is round, but behind lie four square ones which are older. Another engraving from *Earth's Riches* (*c.* 1880), this ironworks can also be seen in the background of the engraving on page 27, illustrating the availability of the raw materials so close to the furnaces.

Nineteenth-century cast iron boundary post. Locally made, it once stood on Turls Hill. BW stands for Ben Whitehouse, whose iron works was at Deepfields, Coseley and who lived at Turls Hill House, Woodsetton. The post was probably cast by the other landowner, whose initials were WP, at the family firm of Ben Parkes at Woodsetton (see opposite).

B. Parkes & Son, Woodsetton Works, Brook Street, 1975. Established in 1839 the firm made fenders, fire irons, ash pans, hat and umbrella stands, range knobs and other miscellaneous castings.

Spring (Vale) Road, Ettingshall, part of Sankey's Manor works, 1979. As cottage industries declined in favour of the larger factory, miscellaneous buildings were often combined. These ones were demolished shortly after this photograph was taken.

Cannon Iron foundries. Founded by the Sheldon brothers in 1826 it lies alongside the canal arm that eventually became Telford's new main line to Birmingham, through Coseley tunnel. These buildings were demolished in the 1980s, and houses now occupy the site. Cannon industries only ceased operating in Coseley in 1994. Until the turn of the century Whitehouse's Priorfield ironworks lay opposite. Then the furnaces went out of blast, and the business closed. The works were demolished in 1908. The chimney bricks were used to build houses in the Rookery area of Lanesfield.

Cannon's old warehouse, Havacre Lane, Coseley. The advertising is directed at passengers on the London Midland and Scottish Railway Stour Valley line. The warehouse was destroyed by fire in 1981.

HOUSES AND

HOMES

*Entrance to the cemetery, Gospel End Street,
Sedgley. This little house was lived in by the Pugh
family, who provided the parish of All Saints with
sextons for generations. Their role included
collecting taxes and the poor rate.*

Dudley Castle. A popular local history society quiz question is 'Which is the oldest dwelling in Sedgley?' The answer is Dudley Castle, for the structure is entirely within the manor in the village of Woodsetton. Fragments of some remaining walls may date from the twelfth century; the keep (above) dates from about 1300. Among the later buildings are a sixteenth-century Renaissance style range, where Queen Elizabeth I would have stayed in 1575, and those in which Mary Queen of Scots may have been imprisoned in 1585.

The beautiful Ellowes Hall was set in impressive parkland just in Lower Gornal in the land west of Ruiton. Built early in the nineteenth century its changing ownership of iron masters reflected the periodic rise and fall of the local industry. Always known locally as The Ellers it was demolished in 1964.

Cotwall End or West Lodge, Ellowes Hall, *c.* 1900. Mr Flavell, the lodge keeper, is in the centre. Left to right are the lodge keeper's wife's sister, Mrs Flavell, their daughter Mrs Edwards, her two sons (one is Robert), and Mr Edwards.

Parkes Hall. The hall was demolished early in the nineteenth century: this painting (1970), by F. Andrew Barnett, is based on a contemporary sketch made during the last days of the hall. The site is now covered by the Parkes Hall reservoir. The Parkes family became much more influential in the manor in about 1600, when Thomas Parker bought the manor from the impoverished Suttons (see page 125).

Gospel End farmhouse. It was demolished in 1966 in error – the contractors had reportedly mistaken it for Sedgley Hall! It had seen many owners and, at the time of this post card, was called Morgan's Farm. It was brick built with a stone façade; although Georgian in appearance, from the back it could be seen that it was of an earlier date and that the façade was an eighteenth-century modernisation. The house stood opposite the entrance to Southerndown Road. Its farmyard wall and gate pillars still remain.

Three-storey house, Gospel End village, 1975. The upper windows show the influence of the Window Tax, which was not repealed until 1851. 'Blind' windows, for ornamental purposes only, avoided taking the owner into the next tax bracket. The house was demolished in 1989.

Townsend House, High Street, Sedgley, 1960. Charles Kemp Homer, grandfather of Frederick Augustus (see page 73), lived here in 1851. Later it became the home of Henry Bickerton Whitehouse, owner of Priorfield ironworks, Deepfields. He also owned coal pits and a factory making firebricks.

Furlongs House, Dudley Road, Upper Gornal, 1973. This impressive Victorian house had several notable owners including the Fullwoods (a prominent local family, who gave their name to Fullwood's End, Coseley) and the Wilkes family (see page 31).

Bleak House, Dudley Road, Upper Gornal. In 1900 it was the home of F.M.A. Powell M.B. Surgeon, Medical Officer and Public Vaccinator Sedgley No.1 district, Dudley Union and Police Surgeon. Most local families remember it in use as 'The Clinic'!

All Saints' Vicarage, Vicar Street. Long thought to be seventeenth-century, evidence of a much older building was found within at its demolition in 1969. The spacious garden is now much reduced in size, owing to the sale of land for development. It was once the scene of many happy occasions, particularly when local children were entertained and given tea to celebrate notable events of the parish.

Ellowes Row, Ruiton, Upper Gornal, 1967. The terrace shows the use of local stone.

Cottages, north side of Gospel End Road, 1935. The high gable walls may well indicate that they were once thatched.

The Grange, Tipton Road, Woodsetton, 1975. It was the home of W.R. Mobberley, a fire-brick manufacturer of Upper Ettingshall, who at one time gloried in the telephone number Sedgley 7.

This little dormer-windowed farmhouse in Hurst Hill survived until 1964, when it was demolished to make way for a housing development.

The so-called Manor House, Bull Ring, Sedgley (see page 10). Residents included Abner Farnworth and George E. Brown, ironmonger and tool seller of Snow Hill, Wolverhampton. The final occupant was Dr Chand, a local GP who vacated the house in 1968. It was demolished some months later.

55 High Street (near Springfield Grove), Sedgley, 1909. Anna Flavell, daughters Louisa and Elizabeth and son Ben gather at the gate of a typical village centre dwelling.

Beacon Passage, Sedgley, early 1970s. This little row stands empty, awaiting demolition.

Section Five

STREETSCAPES

AND ROADS

Children at play in North Street.

Kent Street, Upper Gornal, *c.* 1928. It was called Sheepcot Wall before 1873, indicating a former farming environment.

Clarence Street, Upper Gornal, 1920s. The building on the left is now the Labour Club.

Old Dudley Street, Sedgley, *c*. 1900. A steam tram descends to the Bull Ring.

Gospel End Street, *c*. 1900. It was known as 'Bush Bank' because of the inn of that name that used to stand at the top where the triangular traffic island is today. The footpath entering from the right leaves an old bier way from the parish church which ran behind the houses and headed for Sandyfields.

Looking down Dudley Street to the Bull Ring, 1960s. The Clifton cinema, built in 1937, replaced Hilton and Caswell's builders yard and house, together with Carmi Fox's butcher's shop and abattoir.

Vicar Street, Sedgley, 1970. On the left is the old vestry where the Board of Health was convened after the cholera epidemics of 1832 and 1849. It occupies the site of the tithe barn. All Saints' church is in the background and a classroom of the National School on the right (see page 106).

Gate Street, Sedgley, from Tipton Road, 1960. It was called Old Street before the arrival of the Bunker's Hill toll gate at the bottom, in 1843 (see page 94). The houses on the right have been replaced by new houses.

Dean Street, Sedgley, 1969. This view clearly shows it as the older road to the heart of Sedgley from Wolverhampton. The Bull Ring and the High Street lead naturally from it.

High Street, Sedgley looking towards the Bull Ring, 1968. The miscellany of buildings fronting the Manor House were all demolished to make way for a new shopping block in 1969.

High Street, Sedgley, east side. The Pig and Whistle stands behind the trees and a variety of dwellings and shops complete the street scene to Brick Street corner. The building on the extreme right, in Brick Street, is Hunt the builders, but once housed the Salvation Army. In 1968 demolition began of this part of the High Street in preparation for a by-pass that never came. The photograph was taken shortly before demolition.

Dean Street, Sedgley, 1970s. The photograph was taken from the roof of the north aisle of the church during a roof repair.

Musk Lane, Lower Gornal, 1968. The house on the left is now well below the road surface because of the changes in level brought about by improvements over the years. The house in the centre is probably 'one up and one down'.

North Street, Lower Gornal, 1960s. The houses provide further evidence of the use of local stone. The street, which has now disappeared, ran westwards from Lake Street next to Turner Street.

Straits Green, Lower Gornal, 1920s. St Andrew's Mission church is visible amongst the trees (centre). Yew Tree Cottage, to the right, still stands.

The Priory, Sedgley, seen from Ladies Walk, c. 1965. The priory referred to is that of Dudley, which had received these lands as an endowment from the lord of the manor.

Gospel End village, looking west. The building on the right is the sub-post office. This John Price postcard dates from the 1920s.

The road cutting through the sandstone at Gospel End, 1975. An ancient road, it has always provided an important way west from the manor. References to the widening of the cutting are known from accounts of the sixteenth century.

Gospel End Road looking east from above the rock cutting, 1975. In the middle ground on the left is old Red Lane Farm (see page 21). The steeple of All Saints can be seen on the horizon and the Brownswall Farm fields, in the distance on the right, are already covered by houses.

CHURCHES AND

CHAPELS

Members of Himley Road Wesleyan Band.

The parish church of All Saints, from the west (see page 2). It served all of the nine villages in the manor. Footpaths or bier ways radiated from it to the manor's extremities and remnants of many of them are still in existence today. Many of these field paths could be as much as 900–1,000 years old. The wall-mounted ornamental railings were removed between 1939 and 1944 to aid the war effort.

The church choir, officers and clergy in the front of the old vicarage, during the Second World War. Back row, left to right: -?- (churchwarden), Seth Pugh (verger), Tom Wright, Jack Richards, Mr Cox, Ernie Barratt, A.L. Sherratt, J.W. Hartland, Mr Bullock, Ron Bagley, Mr Billingham (organist), Mr Parnell, Haden Lloyd, Mr Rushton, Bob Shinton, Mr Norton, Jim Wassell, Ben Fullwood, -?-, Mr Williams (churchwarden). Middle row: ? Cotton, Jeremy Gale, Alan Cottam, Pat Allen, Revd Trevor H.H. Kilburn (vicar), Mr Barnes (curate), Nigel Bodenham, Max Robinson, Leonard Marsh, Tony Sherratt, Front row, left to right: Bill Harper, Desmond Foster, Bernard Fownes, Trevor Downing, Alan Harris, Paul Marsh, Tony Braddock.

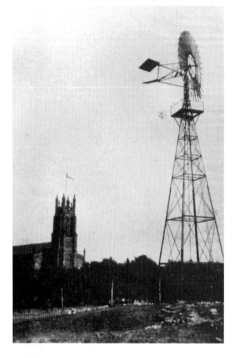

Christchurch, Coseley, *c.* 1920. The nineteenth century saw the established church seeking to combat the effects that population growth and growing industrialisation were having on the effectiveness of the extensive parish system. It did this by building chapels of ease and missions in all parts of the manor. Christchurch, Coseley was such a chapel of ease and was built in 1830. This photograph shows that when electric light came to the church it was powered by its own wind generator.

The first Straits Mission, Lower Gornal, fell prey to mining subsidence. It became such a local novelty that a John Price postcard featured it, early this century. It appears that the stones from a wall which has been demolished have been stacked against the hedge.

St Oswald's mission, Ladymoor, Ettingshall, *c*. 1970. Last used at the end of the 1960s it was demolished in the 1970s. Its bell, seen hanging at the front, is preserved in Sedgley Museum, Brick Street.

The interior of St Oswald's.

Roman Catholic chapels re-entered the parish in the eighteenth century. In 1786 Father Perry added a chapel to his house in Sandyfields. Its name of St George's became synonymous with the tiny hamlet in which it stood. This window is the last surviving remnant of the chapel and is now within a house wall. The hamlet still exists, amongst modern housing along Sandyfields Road.

St Peter and the English Martyrs, 1926. This was the modest forerunner of the present Roman Catholic church in Lower Gornal.

St Chad's and All Saints, late 1920s. Formerly St George's church it was situated at the top of Downing's Lane and was renamed when rebuilt in 1823. This interior view shows it lit by gas: the mantles and shades are mounted on long tubes from the floor.

Providence Baptist chapel, Coseley, 1972. The Baptists had several chapels in the villages of Lower Sedgley. A chapel had been built on this site in 1809. This building dates from 1870 and is still there, although it has been reduced in height.

Chapel, Fir Street, Gospel End. It was built as a Wesleyan chapel in 1846, but has also been a Baptist chapel, in the 1930s. It is now a private residence and has also recently housed a pottery.

Virgin's Row, Lanesfield, Ettingshall. Many of the Nonconformist chapels began as 'cottage' meetings. This little dwelling, the home of Mary Miles, was the birthplace of the congregation of Lanesfield Wesleyan chapel, built in 1834, in Spring (Vale) Road.

Lanesfield Wesleyan chapel, *c.* 1900. The clock tower was removed in the 1920s for fear of subsidence. A tiny wooden bell tower replaced it. To the right stands the chapel of 1834, demolished for a new Sunday School in 1909. On the extreme right is Lanesfield House, built in 1890. The new chapel is already structurally tied against subsidence, with steel bars running the length of the building and bolted with round 'bulls-eye' disc plates at both ends. All of these buildings were demolished in about 1962 when the church moved to Laburnam Road. The two trees by the Wesleyan chapel door, now mature horse chestnuts, still stand in Spring Road.

Ladymoor Wesleyan church, *c.* 1900. It was built in 1848–49 just inside the ancient boundary of Ettingshall village and demolished in 1903, because of subsidence. It stood on the corner of Broadlanes and Highfields Road. The gentleman on the steps is probably Joseph Barnett, a stalwart of local Methodism.

Wesleyan chapel, Kent Street, Upper Gornal. A stone-built chapel, it was demolished, together with its near neighbour (see page 70), at the formation of the new Upper Gornal Methodist church in 1970.

Sedgley Wesleyans purchased Homer's Temperance Hall and Ragged School in the High Street, and moved here from their little chapel in Bilston Street in 1904. This photograph, dating from 1970, shows the improved façade added to the buildings in 1908 (see page 74).

Wesleyan Band, 1907. The Wesleyans of Himley Road, Gornal Wood, bring out their band to help celebrate their Sunday School treat.

Primitive Methodist chapel, Lake Street, Lower Gornal. It was built in about 1840 and was used by the Primitive Methodists until they moved across the road to new premises in 1926. The old chapel became the workshop of Burrows the printer.

Mount Zion, Upper Gornal. This was the home of the New Connection Methodists until they joined Kent Street to form Upper Gornal Methodists on this site in 1970.

Sunday school anniversary choir, Hurst Hill Methodist, late 1940s. Local girls in their white dresses wait at the door of the church to enter. Their choirmaster, seen on the steps, is Mr Cyril Smith. Also on the steps are Miss Sheila Aston (left) and Miss Beryl Swatman.

Sedgley Congregational church, Bilston Street, winter 1970. The Thomas Darbey school is seen to its left.

Himley Road Wesleyan Band – the one seen on page 69?

Homer's new Assembly Hall, Gospel End Street, Sedgley. It was built after the sale of the temperance movement's buildings in the High Street to the Wesleyans, and was photographed shortly after its completion in about 1902.

Frederick A. Homer, one-time self-confessed drunkard, founded the temperance movement in Sedgley in 1859, amongst other works of public benevolence. Here he stands, back row left, with his temperance army, or 'Homer's Army' as they were known, in the 1870s. Back row, left to right: Frederick Homer, Ben Fellows, David Richards, Captain Cox and Brother Haig, Absalom Jukes, David Hyde, Ben Johnson. Front row: Seth Pugh, Joe Shorthouse, Richard Harrison, Jim or Edward Poultney, Job Slater, Jim Siddaway, Ben Cole. Seated on the floor: Ben Wilkes.

An older F.A. Homer stands with some of his family outside the front door of his home, Dormston House, Sedgley. The clergyman is possibly the Revd Thomas G. Swindell. The photograph must have been taken in about 1900, as Homer died in 1901, aged 72.

Homer's original Temperance Hall, *c.* 1900. It is seen here before the façade was added by the Wesleyans (see page 69), after their move from Bilston Street.

Foundation stone, Ragged School and Temperance Hall. It was laid by Eliza Tinsley, the local nail magnate, in 1862. The stone, seen here in its original setting at the rear of the hall, was re-sited in 1983 after the demolition and is now preserved in the foyer of the St Andrew's URC/Methodist community building in Bilston Street.

Section Seven

SHOPS AND
SERVICES

Staff of Marsh's butcher's shop.

Dudley Co-operative Society shop, Bull Ring, Dudley, 1909. In the doorway is Anna Turner, wife of the manager John Turner. The shop became A. Sproson Vinrace's grocery store when the Co-op moved in the 1920s (see page 8).

A later Co-op, High Street, Sedgley. It was housed in this 1922 building between the three-storeyed Mill House and the Midlands Electricity showroom.

Marsh's butcher's shop, Holborn House, Sedgley, 1929. The staff pose with their Model T Ford vans, left to right: Frank Robson, Albert Allen, Thomas Alfred Marsh, Harry Taylor and, leaning on the van, Richard Westwood. Marsh's original shop was in the single-storey addition to his Grand Junction Inn in High Holborn (see page 91). Expansion took them across the road to Holborn House.

'Quality Clothes', Bull Ring, Sedgley, 1952. The 1936 'Flying' Standard 9 belonged to Ron Baker and is parked outside his tailor's shop. Next door is the little grocery shop of the Purcer sisters.

Mrs W. Allen outside her drapery and haberdashery shop in Kent Street, Upper Gornal, early this century.

Griffin's, formerly Smith's, corner shop, Catchem's Corner, Ettingshall. Manor Road, with its pre-1875 housing, runs away on the right. Millfields Road runs left towards Bilston.

Roseville sub-post office, the Square, Coseley.

101 Clifton Street, Hurst Hill, *c.* 1894. Left to right: the Hurst Hill sub-postmaster William Jones, his daughter Florence with Rover, his son Albert Henry, who succeeded him as sub-postmaster, and William's wife Louise. Albert Henry's stepdaughter, Elsie, took over the post office in Can Lane (see page 32) and kept it almost to the end of its life, before it was re-sited across the road.

Sub-post office, High Street, Sedgley. Staff pose proudly in their uniforms early this century. The first sub-postmaster was Mr Bourne, of Bourne House. He is probably the gentleman on the left of the photograph as he was noted for wearing jackboots.

Naylors outfitters, Bilston Street, Sedgley. The proprietor of the shop has a name reminiscent of the old trade at which a distant ancestor had evidently worked. This is the oldest shop in the row and is set obliquely to the road line of Bilston Street.

During this century there were several 'shed' shops in the area. Many will remember this as Hughes the cobbler's at Swan Village, Woodsetton, although it was originally built to serve tobacco and refreshments to travellers using the Birmingham New Road, recently opened.

Jim Hughes at his last inside his well-stocked workshop, 1980s.

Grainger's shop, Bayer Street, Coseley. The name Bayer is either a cartographer's refinement or a misunderstanding of the local dialect. The street is really Bear Street and owes its name to an inn that once stood here.

A one-time 'tommy' or truck shop, Tipton Street, Sedgley. It is opposite a nail factor's warehouse. The factor used the truck shop to pay the outworkers in goods rather than money.

Holborn garage, next to Ladies Walk and the old graveyard, Sedgley, 1960s. Today Safeway occupies the site and the graveyard has been landscaped. The garage had previously been a smithy and belonged at one time to the Johnson family.

This sign for best American lamp oil, lamp wicks, chimneys and burners was, for many years, upon the wall of a building used by the Midlands Electricity Board! (See page 76.) The photograph dates from 1970, and the sign was painted over soon afterwards.

Groucutt Street, Coseley, 1976. Parish relief was paid to Lower Sedgley recipients from this little office from early in the nineteenth century.

This stone title, built into the office, was probably defaced when the Urban District of Coseley came into existence in 1895 and the name Sedgley was thought no longer appropriate.

A stone building in Upper Gornal that survived its intended use by many years. It was the village 'lock-up'! It was demolished in the 1970s.

Section Eight

PUBLIC HOUSES

A group outside the Horse and Jockey.

Seven Stars Inn, Bush Bank, Sedgley. The old inn awaits demolition in 1995. The old Bush Inn, demolished in 1925, stood almost opposite, below the police station.

The Horse and Jockey, Ivy House Lane, Coseley, c. 1910.

The Britannia, Kent Street, Upper Gornal. It is thought to have been built as a row of cottages in the middle of the eighteenth century, one becoming a 'beer house': it received its licence in 1832. It is said that one family ran the Britannia for over a hundred years. Like many others this inn incorporated a butcher's shop (the window on the left). Now the inn occupies the whole building.

The Tilted Barrel, Princes End, Brierley. Its name must have been suitably extended as subsidence took its toll. It still resists collapse!

The Pear Tree, Lower Gornal. This inn takes its name from a well-favoured local garden asset. The small hard pears, sometimes called 'Tettnul Dicks', are very popular with the children. The gasworks in the background is a well-known local landmark.

The Woodman Inn, off Wakelam's Fold, Lower Gornal. The Woodman would have quenched the thirst of many a local nailer and collier but appears to owe its name to an earlier trade.

The Grand Junction Inn, Sedgley. Named after Stephenson's railway that reached Birmingham from Crewe, via Bushbury, Heath Town and Bescot, it was built of local stone when window tax was still in effect. The single-storey butcher's shop of the publican W.H. Marsh (see page 77) can be seen on the extreme right.

The Five Ways Inn, Lower Gornal. Also built from local stone it seems to follow the fashion for having a butcher's shop adjoining.

The Beacon, Beacon Lane, Sedgley, 1971. With its own brewery at the rear it was typical of many where 'home brewing' was considered to be the rule.

The Forge Inn, Lower Gornal, *c*. 1970. Some local public houses bore a name reflecting the local trades. The Forge Hammer at Lanesfield and the Rolling Mill at Millfields are other examples. There are several Boat Inns, and an Anchor along the canal.

Section Nine

TRANSPORT

A tram driver and conductor.

Bunker's Hill Toll House, Sedgley, 1925. Standing outside are, left to right: Mr Jabez Fellows, his son Major and daughters Cissie and Mildred Fellows. The toll house gave Gate Street its name: it stood by the entrance to the present Richmond Road. It was demolished in 1933.

Littleworth Toll House, Woodsetton, 1975. This was next down the line of Tipton Road. The turnpike route was short lived. The toll house built for its opening in 1843 closed, along with all the others, in 1876. It continued to exist as a house, though it has now been completely rebuilt in the Black Country Museum, Dudley.

Wednesbury Oak Loop, Highfields, Brierley. Part of the earliest canal through the manor, it was constructed from Birmingham to Wolverhampton in 1769–72; James Brindley was the engineer. At the time it must have been the best road in the manor for any journey, either for passengers or goods! The tall roof belongs to the Boat Inn.

Bull Ring, Sedgley, *c.* 1900. The view is from the top floor of John Egginton's shop. A double-decker steam tram car is pulled by its locomotive towards Wolverhampton. It passes the Manor House garden wall.

Erection of the electric tram poles, Bull Ring, Sedgley, *c*. 1900. There was still a continuing dependence upon horses. The house on the left is that of Carmi Fox who owned a butcher's shop and abattoir. Clifton cinema, built in 1937, replaced it.

Erection of the electric tram poles, Bull Ring, Sedgley, *c*. 1900. In 1901 the electric trams commenced running to be replaced by trolley buses in the 1920s. The poles erected here served both and, last of all, provided the standards for the street lighting until the 1960s.

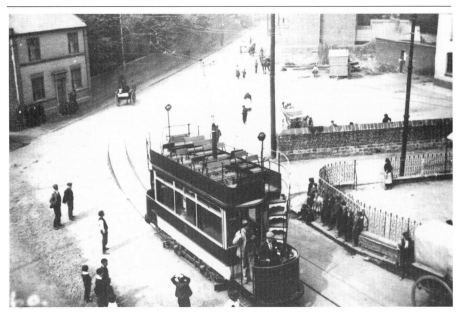

Bull Ring, Sedgley, *c.* 1901. This is an early arrival of the electric tram in Sedgley taken from the top floor of John Egginton's shop (see page 96). Notice how the spectators gather to see it.

This electric tram has turned from the Parkfield Road at Fighting Cocks Inn, and waits to continue its journey towards Dudley, on the route from Willenhall and Bilston.

Bull Ring, Sedgley, *c.* 1901. The house next to Egginton's was once the residence of a Sedgley doctor. It later became a shop (see page 8).

A detail of the tram pole base, showing the distinctive badge of the local tram companies of Birmingham and district, in this case the WDET (Wolverhampton & District Electric Tramways Co. Ltd). Some of these tram poles were still being used as street lighting standards in the early 1970s. This one was photographed in Clarence Street, Upper Gornal, in 1971.

Horses remained important for road goods, particularly in Upper Gornal and Ruiton. The Watton and the Harper families both used the traditional carts. These carts travelled many miles delivering salt and hardware goods; the family would make the cart their home during the journey. This photograph, taken in 1922, shows William Harper with an agricultural fork; he sold various tools and buckets to Midlands farmers. Also pictured are his wife Anne and their daughter Annie.

An earlier photograph of the family. They have paused in a field at Brewood and Mrs Harper is doing some washing. The little boy was not a member of the family, but had been allowed to climb up on the cart.

Homeward bound in Ruiton, Upper Gornal, *c.* 1975. A tired horse returns with his owner, possibly Charles Watton, who is carrying the fodder. They are probably returning from a long journey selling salt.

Visit of the Prince of Wales, Coseley, November 1927. The opening of the Birmingham New Road to Wolverhampton cut the manor in two. Here the entourage accompanying the Prince of Wales, on the official opening day, passes the Ebenezer Baptist church at Coseley.

Bull Ring, Sedgley, *c.* 1900. The solitary cyclist would be amazed to know the busy traffic centre that the road would become.

Today the former dependence upon horses is shown by the surviving 'pitching rings' in stable and coach house gable ends. They were a common feature of stables and coach houses, providing easy access for hay or straw from outside. Hay was pitched from the top of a cart with a hay fork, and was then stored in the upper chamber. Provision was made in the upper floor for it to be dropped through as required. This one, photographed in 1976, became a window when the building was converted to a house shortly afterwards.

Trolley buses, Dudley Street, Sedgley, 1967. Trolley buses had replaced trams in the area during the 1920s. By 1967 they too were being replaced.

Section Ten

EDUCATION

Pupils learning craft skills.

Sedgley National School was built in 1828 upon what had once been part of the village green. A classroom stands on either side of the school house. Both photographs were taken shortly before the school's demolition in 1966.

The commemorative stone showing the benevolence of the Earl of Dudley in providing the school. His ownership is shown in no uncertain terms!

Thomas Darbey School, Bilston Street, Sedgley, 1970. It was built in 1861, partly at his expense, alongside the Congregational church. The Foster Education Act of 1870 later resulted in the creation of the Board schools.

Christchurch Infants School, Coseley. It received its first grant funding in 1832.

Lanesfield, Wood Street, was one of the Board schools of the parish. Built in 1879, it was extended in 1894 when the classrooms in the foreground were built. They were divided internally by wood and glass partitions that opened up to make a large hall. The photograph dates from 1924.

Lanesfield, Wood Street, 1905. The headmaster, Thomas Brecknell, poses with the class.

A class party at Lanesfield to celebrate the coronation of Queen Elizabeth in 1953. Amongst the children are Barry Farley and Beric Elwell.

It appears that only girls at Lanesfield were encouraged in craft skills in 1935! The doorway to the right, beyond the wall, had 'Am I clean and early' carved into the stone lintel. Back row, left to right: Dorothy Westwood (?), Audrey Flavell, Peggy Deakin, Olive Jones, Kathleen Butler, Lydia Gilks, Maud Boucker, -?-, Sylvia Genge. Middle row: Mildred Smith, Millicent Baugh, -?-, -?-. Front row: Peggy Ward, -?-, Jean Richards, Barbara Phillips, Sheila Oakley, Dorothy Phillips, -?-, -?-, Nora Sheldon.

Staff, Tudor Boys School, Upper Gornal, c. 1930. Standing, left to right: H. Baker (?), E. Howes, R. Price (standing behind his father). Seated: R. Knott, W.H. Potts (headmaster), S. Price.

The 'Tin' school, Broadlanes, Coseley, 1922. The headmaster, in the centre, was James M. Wright. Other members of staff were Mr Moody, Mr Hopcut, Miss Stanley, Miss Fellows and Mr Millard.

Broadlanes football team, 1921. They were the proud Coseley schools' cup winners.

Mount Pleasant Board school, Coseley, 1929. Top row, left to right: A. Fry, A. Lockley, B. Mayo, V. Aston, J. Smallman, W. Flavell, F. Jones, H. Whitehouse, L. Hale. Second row: Abraham Hartill (headmaster), R. Winsor, M. Bailey, D. Dodd, D. Groucutt, W. Squires, D. Flavell, L. Johnson, O. Hollis, M. Hockle, F. Porter, Miss Haigh (teacher). Third row: B. Smith, D. Blower, L. Harper, E. Cook, V. Haynes, M. Pearson, H. Attwell, N. Briscoe, K. Plimmer, V. Porter, J. Webb, G. Harper. Fourth row: Ron Baker, H. Flavell, R. Jones, F. Caddick, M. White, D. Webb, J. White, H. Bourne, A. Smith. Front row: S. Houseman, A. Flavell, H. Fieldhouse, L. Jay, J. Flavell, C. Fownes, D. Haywood, T. Slater.

Section Eleven

LIFE AND LEISURE

Cast members of The Mikado.

In what is probably Sedgley's most famous picture, a dancing bear performs in the Bull Ring, in front of Hilton's, *c.* 1901. After the performance had ended, the show would probably have moved on to the Jockey Fields in Upper Gornal. The traffic island here, with its single lamp standard, has grown in size to its modern proportions to handle present traffic conditions.

A more refined pursuit on the lawn of Dormston House, Dudley Street, Sedgley, at the turn of the century. Frederick Homer and his family indulge in a game of croquet (see page 73). All Saints' church is in the background on this sunny evening. Notice the parrot in a gilded cage that has been brought out for a breath of air!

High Street Methodists perform *The Mikado*, *c.* 1938. Fred Wilkes (president) stands at the far left. At the other end of that row stands William I. Slater, pianist and headmaster of Queen Victoria Junior School. Also in the picture are W.I. Slater's wife Evelyn, Neville K. Price, grandson of John Price of Bilston, Fred Slater, Lily Camm, Arthur Slater (brother of Fred) and his wife Lucy.

The unveiling of the statue of Dr Baker, Hurst Hill, 1914. The area has always owed much to its doctors, who often worked without fees from those who could not afford to pay. Francis Brett Young wrote about such a personality in *Dr Bradley Remembers*, which is set in Sedgley. The cost of this statue was met by local public subscription from a grateful populace. Back row, left to right: -?-, John W. Baker (draper of Hollywell Street), S.K. Slater JP, Mr Dunton (Hurst Hill Board School headmaster), Albert Sherwin (rate collector), Albert Screen, Mr Cooper, Mr Swann (of the Miners Arms), Mr Golby (policeman). Front row: Mr Waterhouse (screw manufacturer), K. Fellows, Revd A. Holling (minister of Bilston Street Congregational church, Sedgley), Mr Pugh, Mr Etheridge (coal merchant), Samuel Wasdell (of The Boat Inn, Hurst Road).

A John Price postcard of Baggeridge Woods, Gospel End, 1920s. One of the 'lungs' of the area, Sedgley folk were always to be found here. Many holidays were spent in the woods and Saturday and Sunday evening walks persisted for many years.

A postcard from the same series, featuring the Wishing Pool. A local custom was to stand on a particular stone at the water's edge, with your back to the pool, throw a penny over your shoulder and make a wish.

Monument, Sedgley Beacon. Yet another walk was to the Monument, scene of beacon fires since the Armada. Here the views over the Black Country to the east and the rural countryside of Shropshire to the west make a striking contrast even today.

Dog breeding has retained its popularity although the cruel use of them has passed. Here these two proud breeders pose with their Staffordshire bull terrier.

A Gornal dog show now provides the competitive element for the breeders. The participants are lined up outside The Woodman Inn, Wakelam's Fold, 1970s.

An enigmatic photograph from the beginning of this century shows an important procession marching into Sedgley Bull Ring, led by the Sedgley town band. Again it was taken from the top floor of John Egginton's shop (see pages 96 and 98). There have been many suggestions as to the occasion. One asserts that it was an important wedding party walking to church; certainly there is a bride-like figure with veil blowing in the wind. It has also been suggested that it was an anniversary or patronal festival procession. Another feasible explanation is linked with the work of F.A. Homer again (see page 73): perhaps the temperance queen had been chosen for the year and was being processed around the village and to church.

Home Guard Divisional officers in front of Dormston House, 1943. Back row, left to right: Lt. A. Sherratt, 2/Lt. R. Greenwood, Lt. S. Wheeler, Lt. G. Palmer, 2/Lt. A. Davis, Lt. D. Morris, 2/Lt. W. Wellings, 2/Lt. S Watton, Lt. S. Wright, 2/Lt L. Holmes, Lt G. Lane. Third row: 2/Lt. D. Reid, Lt. K. Powis, 2/Lt C. Clements, 2/Lt. K. Hart, Lt. J. Ratcliffe, Lt. R. White, Lt. W. Edwards, Lt. E. Adams, Lt. D. Greenaway, Lt. H. Hendrick, 2/Lt. W. Price, Lt. A. Winwood. Seated: Capt. J. Bradshaw, Capt. C. Bathurst, Capt. S. Beresford, Major A. Jeavons, Major W. Wootton, Major G. Ward, Lt. Col. G.R. Sankey, Major E. Walker, Major J. Aston, Capt. A. Oliver, Capt. E. Bent, Capt. A. Pugh. Front row: Lt. F. Rogers, Lt. R. Shaw, Lt. J. Cholmondeley, Lt. J. McCracken, Lt. H. Perry, Lt. R. Johnstone, 2/Lt. F. Meachem, Lt. A. Martin.

Formerly Jack Darby's Picture House, Upper Gornal. It was one of the early entrants into the world of the silver screen. The tram depot lay right behind. By the time of this photograph, in 1965, it had became a DIY store.

Hill Avenue, Lanesfield, late 1940s. This was one of the first playgrounds for children built after the Second World War. It is a sign of a growing concern for the loss of natural play space for the young brought about by the increase in building.

Round Hill limeworks and quarry, Sedgley Beacon. Nature has reclaimed the limeworks and quarry (see page 24), which have become a playground and source of fossils to local children. The site has now been declared a Site of Special Scientific Interest.

Construction of the underground reservoir, Sedgley Beacon, 1970. Another milestone! In operation from 1972, the reservoir led to the removal of the water tanks that had been a local landmark since 1922.

Queen Elizabeth II passing through Sedgley, 1977. The queen passed through Sedgley and Upper Gornal on her Jubilee tour. No doubt there was some expense incurred by the local authority, but much less penalising than when Queen Elizabeth I came to stay with the Suttons at Dudley Castle in Sedgley. Then, it is said, the family became so impoverished that the manor had to be sold to the Parkes family of Willingsworth (Wednesbury) (see page 42). The greatest misfortune to have happened to Sedgley in 1977 is that *Rocky* appears to have caused L to be knocked out of the Clifton!

Acknowledgements

I should like to acknowledge my use of the following sources:
The Black Country Society • Dudley Library Archives and Local History Service • Wolverhampton Public Library Archives and Local History Service Sedgley Local History Society and Museum members • Lanesfield Primary School • The late E. Foulkes • The late F. Andrew Barnett.

Also the following, who have so readily provided me with personal photographs or information:

Howard Briscoe • Ron Davies • Walter Goldie • Hetty Naylor • Neville Price Dorothy Johnson • Graham Furnival • William (Bill) Marsh • H. Nicholls Elsie Williams • Kath Oseland • William Burgess • Mrs E. Morgan • May Simner Cyril Field • Frank Jones • Mrs Hickling • John Legg • Dennis Baker A.H. Price • Joe and Mary Harper.

I should wish to acknowledge particularly the contributions of Angela Kiely, for her acquisition of several photographs, information and help with text, and to Ron Baker for photographs from his personal collection and for finding so many people who possessed such treasured illustrations of our past.

Every effort has been made to contact all copyright holders of photographs where copyright has not originated with the person owning them.

THE BLACK COUNTRY SOCIETY

This voluntary society, affiliated to the Civic Trust, was founded in 1967 as a reaction to the trend of the late 1950s and early 1960s to amalgamate everything into large units and in the Midlands to sweep away the area's industrial heritage in the process.

The general aim of the Society is to create interest in the past, present and future of the Black Country, and early on it campaigned for the establishment of an industrial museum. In 1975 the Black Country Museum was started by Dudley Borough Council on 26 acres of totally derelict land adjoining the grounds of Dudley Castle. This has developed into an award-winning museum which attracts over 250,000 visitors annually.

There are over two thousand members of the Black Country Society and all receive the quarterly magazine *The Blackcountryman*, of which over 105 issues have been published since its founding in 1967. In the whole collection there are some 1,500 authoritative articles on all aspects of the Black Country by historians, teachers, researchers, students, subject experts and ordinary folk with an extraordinary story to tell. The whole constitutes a unique resource about the area and is a mine of information for students and researchers who frequently refer to it. Many schools and libraries are subscribers. Three thousands copies of the magazine are printed each quarter. It is non-commercial, and contributors do not receive payment for their articles.

PO Box 71 · Kingswinford · West Midlands DY6 9YN

BRITAIN IN OLD PHOTOGRAPHS

To order any of these titles please telephone Littlehampton Book Services on 01903 721596

Scunthorpe, *D Taylor*
Skegness, *W Kime*
Around Skegness, *W Kime*

LONDON

Balham and Tooting, *P Loobey*
Crystal Palace, Penge & Anerley, *M Scott*
Greenwich and Woolwich, *K Clark*
Hackney: A Second Selection, *D Mander*
Lewisham and Deptford, *J Coulter*
Lewisham and Deptford: A Second Selection, *J Coulter*
Streatham, *P Loobey*
Around Whetstone and North Finchley, *J Heathfield*
Woolwich, *B Evans*

MONMOUTHSHIRE

Chepstow and the River Wye, *A Rainsbury*
Monmouth and the River Wye, *Monmouth Museum*

NORFOLK

Great Yarmouth, *M Teun*
Norwich, *M Colman*
Wymondham and Attleborough, *P Yaxley*

NORTHAMPTONSHIRE

Around Stony Stratford, *A Lambert*

NOTTINGHAMSHIRE

Arnold and Bestwood, *M Spick*
Arnold and Bestwood: A Second Selection, *M Spick*
Changing Face of Nottingham, *G Oldfield*
Mansfield, *Old Mansfield Society*
Around Newark, *T Warner*
Nottingham: 1944–1974, *D Whitworth*
Sherwood Forest, *D Ottewell*
Victorian Nottingham, *M Payne*

OXFORDSHIRE

Around Abingdon, *P Horn*
Banburyshire, *M Barnett & S Gosling*
Burford, *A Jewell*
Around Didcot and the Hagbournes, *B Lingham*
Garsington, *M Gunther*
Around Henley-on-Thames, *S Ellis*
Oxford: The University, *J Rhodes*
Thame to Watlington, *N Hood*
Around Wallingford, *D Beasley*
Witney, *T Worley*
Around Witney, *C Mitchell*
Witney District, *T Worley*
Around Woodstock, *J Bond*

POWYS

Brecon, *Brecknock Museum*
Welshpool, *E Bredsdorff*

SHROPSHIRE

Shrewsbury, *D Trumper*
Whitchurch to Market Drayton, *M Morris*

SOMERSET

Bath, *J Hudson*
Bridgwater and the River Parrett, *R Fitzhugh*
Bristol, *D Moorcroft & N Campbell-Sharp*
Changing Face of Keynsham,
  B Lowe & M Whitehead

Chard and Ilminster, *G Gosling & F Huddy*
Crewkerne and the Ham Stone Villages,
  G Gosling & F Huddy
Around Keynsham and Saltford, *B Lowe & T Brown*
Midsomer Norton and Radstock, *C Howell*
Somerton, Ilchester and Langport, *G Gosling & F Huddy*
Taunton, *N Chipchase*
Around Taunton, *N Chipchase*
Wells, *C Howell*
Weston-Super-Mare, *S Poole*
Around Weston-Super-Mare, *S Poole*
West Somerset Villages, *K Houghton & L Thomas*

STAFFORDSHIRE

Aldridge, *J Farrow*
Bilston, *E Rees*
Black Country Transport: Aviation, *A Brew*
Around Burton upon Trent, *G Sowerby & R Farman*
Bushbury, *A Chatwin, M Mills & E Rees*
Around Cannock, *M Mills & S Belcher*
Around Leek, *R Poole*
Lichfield, *H Clayton & K Simmons*
Around Pattingham and Wombourne, *M Griffiths,*
  P Leigh & M Mills
Around Rugeley, *T Randall & J Anslow*
Smethwick, *J Maddison*
Stafford, *J Anslow & T Randall*
Around Stafford, *J Anslow & T Randall*
Stoke-on-Trent, *I Lawley*
Around Tamworth, *R Sulima*
Around Tettenhall and Codsall, *M Mills*
Tipton, Wednesbury and Darlaston, *R Pearson*
Walsall, *D Gilbert & M Lewis*
Wednesbury, *I Bott*
West Bromwich, *R Pearson*

SUFFOLK

Ipswich: A Second Selection, *D Kindred*
Around Ipswich, *D Kindred*
Around Mildenhall, *C Dring*
Southwold to Aldeburgh, *H Phelps*
Around Woodbridge, *H Phelps*

SURREY

Cheam and Belmont, *P Berry*
Croydon, *S Bligh*
Dorking and District, *K Harding*
Around Dorking, *A Jackson*
Around Epsom, *P Berry*
Farnham: A Second Selection, *J Parratt*
Around Haslemere and Hindhead, *T Winter & G Collyer*
Richmond, *Richmond Local History Society*
Sutton, *P Berry*

SUSSEX

Arundel and the Arun Valley, *J Godfrey*
Bishopstone and Seaford, *P Pople & P Berry*
Brighton and Hove, *J Middleton*
Brighton and Hove: A Second Selection, *J Middleton*
Around Crawley, *M Goldsmith*
Hastings, *P Haines*
Hastings: A Second Selection, *P Haines*
Around Haywards Heath, *J Middleton*
Around Heathfield, *A Gillet & B Russell*
Around Heathfield: A Second Selection,
  A Gillet & B Russell
High Weald, *B Harwood*
High Weald: A Second Selection, *B Harwood*
Horsham and District, *T Wales*

Lewes, *J Middleton*
RAF Tangmere, *A Saunders*
Around Rye, *A Dickinson*
Around Worthing, *S White*

WARWICKSHIRE

Along the Avon from Stratford to Tewkesbury, *J Jeremiah*
Bedworth, *J Burton*
Coventry, *D McGrory*
Around Coventry, *D McGrory*
Nuneaton, *S Clews & S Vaughan*
Around Royal Leamington Spa, *J Cameron*
Around Royal Leamington Spa: A Second Selection,
  J Cameron
Around Warwick, *R Booth*

WESTMORLAND

Eden Valley, *J Marsh*
Kendal, *M & P Duff*
South Westmorland Villages, *J Marsh*
Westmorland Lakes, *J Marsh*

WILTSHIRE

Around Amesbury, *P Daniels*
Chippenham and Lacock, *A Wilson & M Wilson*
Around Corsham and Box, *A Wilson & M Wilson*
Around Devizes, *D Buxton*
Around Highworth, *G Tanner*
Around Highworth and Faringdon, *G Tanner*
Around Malmesbury, *A Wilson*
Marlborough: A Second Selection, *P Colman*
Around Melksham,
  Melksham and District Historical Association
Nadder Valley, *R. Sawyer*
Salisbury, *P Saunders*
Salisbury: A Second Selection, *P Daniels*
Salisbury: A Third Selection, *P Daniels*
Around Salisbury, *P Daniels*
Swindon: A Third Selection, *The Swindon Society*
Swindon: A Fourth Selection, *The Swindon Society*
Trowbridge, *M Marshman*
Around Wilton, *P Daniels*
Around Wootton Bassett, Cricklade and Purton, *T Sharp*

WORCESTERSHIRE

Evesham to Bredon, *F Archer*
Around Malvern, *K Smith*
Around Pershore, *M Dowty*
Redditch and the Needle District, *R Saunders*
Redditch: A Second Selection, *R Saunders*
Around Tenbury Wells, *D Green*
Worcester, *M Dowty*
Around Worcester, *R Jones*
Worcester in a Day, *M Dowty*
Worcestershire at Work, *R Jones*

YORKSHIRE

Huddersfield: A Second Selection, *H Wheeler*
Huddersfield: A Third Selection, *H Wheeler*
Leeds Road and Rail, *R Vickers*
Pontefract, *R van Riel*
Scarborough, *D Coggins*
Scarborough's War Years, *R Percy*
Skipton and the Dales, *Friends of the Craven Museum*
Around Skipton-in-Craven, *Friends of the Craven Museum*
Yorkshire Wolds, *I & M Sumner*